Robins

Julie Murray

Peachtree

Abdo
EVERYDAY ANIMALS
Kids

abdopublishing.com

Published by Abdo Kids, a division of ABDO, PO Box 398166, Minneapolis, Minnesota 55439.
Copyright © 2016 by Abdo Consulting Group, Inc. International copyrights reserved in all countries.
No part of this book may be reproduced in any form without written permission from the publisher.

Printed in the United States of America, North Mankato, Minnesota.

102015
012016

Photo Credits: iStock, Shutterstock

Production Contributors: Teddy Borth, Jennie Forsberg, Grace Hansen

Design Contributors: Candice Keimig, Dorothy Toth

Library of Congress Control Number: 2015941762

Cataloging-in-Publication Data

Murray, Julie.

 Robins / Julie Murray.

   p. cm. -- (Everyday animals)

ISBN 978-1-68080-118-7 (lib. bdg.)

Includes index.

1. Robins--Juvenile literature.   I. Title.

598.8--dc23

                         2015941762

Table of Contents

Robins

Robins are birds. We see them in trees.

4

Robins have feathers.

Their bellies are orange.

6

Their wings are dark gray.

They have white **patches**.

Their beaks are yellow.

They have black eyes.
White rings are around
their eyes.

Robins build nests. They use twigs and grass. They also use feathers and mud.

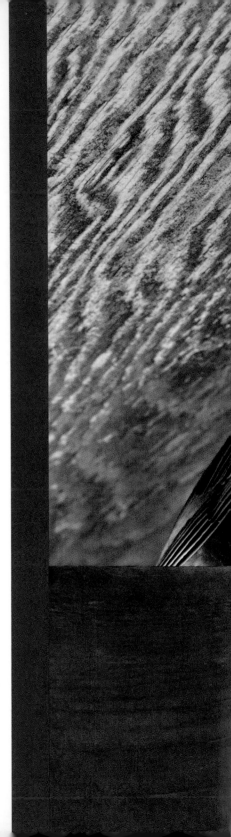

13

They eat berries and bugs.

They even eat worms!

Robins are **songbirds**.

We can hear robins sing.

Robin eggs are easy to spot.

They are light blue!

Have you seen a robin?

Features of a Robin

beak and eyes

orange feathers

light blue eggs

wings and tail feathers

Glossary

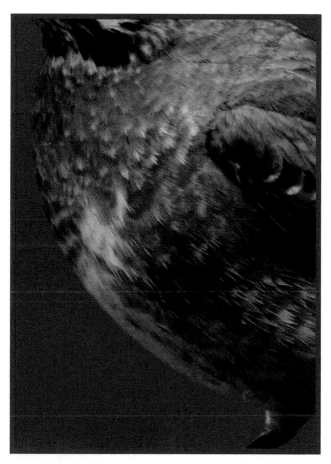

patches
small spots.

songbird
a bird that sings.

Index

abdokids.com

Use this code to log on to abdokids.com and access crafts, games, videos, and more!